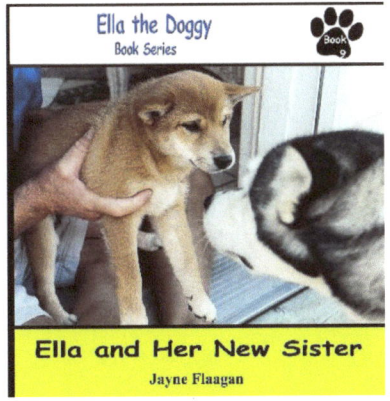

"*Ella and her New Sister*" is dedicated to my "great" niece, *Lily*, who spent time visiting with me, just after welcoming her THIRD sister into her family!

Jayne Flaagan

Husky Publishing
East Grand Forks, MN 56721
Email: djflaagan@gra.midco.net

Copyright © 2021 Jayne Flaagan Cover Design
© 2021 Jayne Flaagan
Photography by Jayne Flaagan

No part of this publication may be reproduced in whole or in part, or stored in a retrieval system, or transmitted in any form or by any means, electronic, mechanical, photocopying, recording or otherwise, without written permission of the author and publisher.

One summer afternoon, Ella was relaxing in the back yard.
She was so comfortable she almost fell asleep.

Suddenly, she heard some strange sounds coming from the house.

Her eyes popped wide open and she quickly got up to find out who was making the noises.

What do you look like when your eyes "pop wide open?"

When Ella got to the back door, a
very big surprise was waiting for her.

Her people friends were holding a new baby puppy!

Ella heard them calling the puppy "Mayme,"

Ella got closer to Mayme to sniff her...
and Mayme wanted to know about Ella too,
so she sniffed Ella right back!

Why do dogs sniff everything?

Before long, everyone went to play in the back yard.
Ella wondered why the puppy was getting so much attention.

What does it mean to "*pay attention*" to someone?

Why was everyone so excited about the puppy?

People were taking lots and lots of pictures of Mayme...

and she even got to crawl in their laps to get extra scratches and hugs!

Why can't Ella crawl on top of people?

Ella started to wonder if anyone still loved her...

Don't worry Ella!

Everyone still loves you just as much as they love Mayme!

After a while, Ella decided to find
a good spot to relax by herself.

But when she turned around, Mayme was following her!

Why do you think Mayme wanted to follow Ella?

Mayme followed Ella *all* day long,
watching *every* single thing she did.

Ella wondered if Mayme would
ever go back to her own home!

"Okay," Ella finally told Mayme, "you can stay for now, but while you are in **MY** yard, you have to be a good girl!"

Mayme quickly rolled onto her back to let Ella know she would behave.

(That's what dogs do when they know someone else is the boss!)

When Mayme saw Ella chewing on a bone,
she licked her lips and decided she wanted a bone too.

Have you ever wanted something
that belonged to someone else?

Look at Mayme! She found an even bigger bone!

How do you think Ella feels about Mayme having that big bone?

Ella wanted to spend some time by herself,
so she went under the deck to hide from Mayme.

When Ella came out from under the deck later, she did not see Mayme.

"*Oh Good, she must have finally gone home,*" she thought.

But then Mayme peeked her head out
from underneath the steps...

(Can you see her?)

Mayme was little, so she did not know to climb steps yet...

but she wanted to reach the top, so she did not give up.

Mayme *worked*,

and *worked*,

and *worked*...

until she reached the very top step!

Good job Mayme!

When it was time for dinner,
can you guess who beat Ella to the door?

Ella did not push Mayme out of the way, though.
Mayme was little and Ella did not want to hurt her.

"Oh well," thought Ella.
"At least I don't have to share my bowl!"

What do you like to share with others?

When it was time for Ella's walk that night,
Mayme was *still* there!

Ella was thinking, "Mmm, maybe
my home *is* going to be Mayme's home too!"

During their walk, Mayme did her best to keep up with Ella.

Why was it hard for Mayme to keep up with Ella?

Mayme did everything Ella did that day, even when Ella climbed a hill!

During their walk, Mayme saw a **VERY** large water bowl!

"No," said Ella.

"This is a river and you must stay back so you don't fall in."

Mayme listened and stayed behind Ella, where it was safe.

Something else Mayme learned was that you need to look both ways before crossing a street or road.

Ella taught Mayme lots of other things too,

like not touching things that might be hot. ..

not to chew on things, like towels...

or pillows...

and especially not people's hats!

Silly Mayme.
(She thinks if she closes her eyes,
no one can see what she has done!)

When it was time for bed, Ella had another surprise.
That little dog Mayme was in **her** bed!

She wanted her to feel at home,
so Ella let Mayme have her sleeping spot.

Wasn't that a nice thing for Ella to do?

The next day, Ella and Mayme went on another walk.
This time, Ella walked slower so Mayme could keep up with her.

Have you ever seen your own shadow?

Ella knew Mayme still had lots of things to learn,

like not getting your head stuck in small spaces...

how to play "*Hide and Seek*"...

not to bite people...

and how to fetch a ball.

(Mayme did not know she was supposed to bring the ball back!)

What does the word "*fetch*" mean?

Can puppies learn their ABC's
so they can play games with people?

What are your favorite games?

Ella knew things would change at home
because she had a new sister.
She did not mind, though.

She still got "*alone time*" with her friends...

and Mayme found that she liked *her own* quiet times too.

Sometimes Ella even gets held like a baby puppy.

And that's okay!

The two sisters found out
it was fun to do things together too.

Like getting belly rubs...

having someone to play with...

and especially going on treasure hunts together!

But of *all* the things Ella and Mayme learned, they found out the *best thing of all* is having someone to look after you.

Especially when it is your own brother or sister!

Jayne Flaagan grew up in North Dakota and now lives in Minnesota with her husband and her goofy dogs, Ella and Mayme. She also has three adult children.

Flaagan's experience includes a background of over 30 years in Elementary and Early Childhood education, as well as an extensive expertise in writing for many different publications and in several different genres. She thoroughly enjoys writing books for young readers!

Books have always been a huge part of the author's life, and reading to children is something she feels is critical to every child's learning experience. Flaagan estimates she has probably read thousands of books to children over the years!

The author grew up on a farm with a Husky and has many fond memories of him. Huskies are fun, lovable and have lots of energy! Ella has provided so much joy and entertainment for her own family, that Flaagan decided she wanted to share her with other families. Thus, "***Ella the Doggy***" book series was born!

"***Ella and her New Sister***" is the first, and only book, (to date) with both Ella and Mayme included in the story!

www.ingramcontent.com/pod-product-compliance
Lightning Source LLC
LaVergne TN
LVHW072054070426
835508LV00002B/88